PRAISE FOR ANDREA GIBSON

"Gibson expertly walks the line between grief and hope, giving readers a deeply layered collection. . . . With all the grace and hope that fans of Gibson's work have come to expect, the author finds beauty even in the most painful moments of their life."

—Ronnie K. Stephens, *Lambda Literary*

"Andrea Gibson's unabashedly emotional poetry performances create communal spaces for audiences to feel through the pain and joy of being queer, express queer love, and break the isolation of mental illness. None of this emotional power is lost in the transition from stage to page. . . . Their work is full of transformations—the lighter beneath a crack spoon becomes dripping ice cream—and witnessing these transformations offers liberation and healing."

—Elizabeth Hoover, *Star Tribune*

"Andrea Gibson's poetry surges on a wave of perseverance. Even as their poems reckon with depression and political turmoil, there's a thread of possibility and hope within them—it may be unraveling, but it's there, and Gibson wants you to take note."

—Caitlin Wolper, *Nylon*

LORD OF THE BUTTERFLIES

poems by

Andrea Gibson

Button Publishing Inc.

Minneapolis

2018

LORD OF THE BUTTERFLIES
POETRY
AUTHOR: Andrea Gibson
COVER DESIGN: Nikki Clark
COVER ART: Cat Rocketship

❖

❖

Published by Button Poetry
Minneapolis, MN 55418 | http://www.buttonpoetry.com

❖

Manufactured in the United States of America
PRINT ISBN: 978-1-943735-42-6
EBOOK ISBN: 978-1-943735-43-3
AUDIOBOOK ISBN: 978-1-63834-035-5

Eighth printing

For my sister.

TABLE OF CONTENTS

LORD OF THE BUTTERFLIES

YOUR LIFE

It isn't that you don't like boys.
It's that you only like boys you want to be:

David, with his jaw carved
out of the side of a cliff.

Malcolm, who doesn't have secrets,
just stories he owes no one.

Chris, the basketball hero with a tic,
blinks fifteen times when he makes a shot.

You spend hours blinking in the mirror, wishing
you could be a star like him.

Mary Levine calls you a dyke
and you don't have the language to tell her she's wrong

and right. You just show up to her house
promising to paint your fingernails red

with what will gush from her busted face
if she ever says it again.

You're in the 7th grade. You don't even know you want a girlfriend.
You still believe in the people who believe in Jesus,

can't even feel that desire
through its hell threat.

You just want to kick your desk on the way to the principal's office,
slouch in detention, cut your hair and spit

out whatever you don't want in your mouth,
your own name even, skirting around the truth.

You don't yet know the boys
are building their confidence on stolen land,

but you worry the girls might be occupied
with things you will never understand,

won't ever be good at. You take one pretty step
and feel like you're pouring bubbles

into your own bloodbath. You don't want a soft death.
You want a hard life that is your life.

Your life in that locker room that doesn't stop demanding
you keep your eyes on the floor.

Your life at the prom where you'll run home
in a snowstorm, chucking your last pair of heels

in a snowbank, realizing you are the only boy
you ever wanted to tear your dress off for.

Your life the first Christmas you spend alone. The years you learn
to build your family from scratch.

Your life the first time someone drags you
from a restroom by the collar of your coat.

Your life each time airport security screams,
Pink or blue? Pink or blue? trying to figure out

which machine setting to run you through.
Choosing your life

and how that made you into someone
who now finds it easy

to explain your gender by saying you are happiest
on the road, when you're not here or there, but in-between,

that yellow line coming down the center of it all
like a goddamn sunbeam.

Your name is not a song you will sing under your breath.
Your pronouns haven't even been invented yet.

You're going to shave your head
and drive through Texas.

You're going to kill your own god
so you can fall in love for the first time.

They're going to keep telling you
your heartbeat is a preexisting condition.

They're going to keep telling you
you are crime of nature.

You're going to look at all of your options
and choose conviction.

Choose to carve your own heart out
of the side of a cliff.

Choose to spend your whole life telling secrets you owe no one
to everyone, until there isn't anyone who can insult you

by calling you what you are:
you holy blinking star.

You highway streak of light
falling over and over for your hard life,

your perfect life,
your sweet and beautiful life.

IVY

After the wound of us scabbed
into polite text, after
we'd charmed each other enough
to wonder if we'd made a mistake,
you invited me to your new apartment
on a night each of us was suffering
from the unbearable loneliness
of sanity.

You had moved to your favorite building
in the city--an almost castle, historic and grand,
wrapped with a century of ivy.
When you opened the door
I was startled by the beauty
of what could be made without me--
a library of books organized by color.
Patti Smith hanging like a Christ
above the checkered tile.
A row of silver knives
you'd finally saved enough to buy, shining
on your kitchen's hand.

You sliced heirloom tomatoes
and made a dressing from scratch
while I eyed the cowhide rug
whose murder I never allowed
in our house. But here, almost free,
almost alive.

After dinner a song came on the stereo
that had been sent to me by another woman
who wore the same red lipstick as you,
but who wasn't like you: chain smoking bartender

reaching for the rifle when the bar fight breaks out,
tattoos you told the artist to scar
on purpose because you couldn't let go
of the guilt of being 800 miles away
when New Orleans drowned, pores sweating bourbon
in the yoga class you cursed through.
I called you a hipster once and you flattened
every bike tire in town with your *fuck no.*

The hours passed smooth as the wine
we downed--like we were pouring the blood
back into our bodies.
I could have driven home
but we both said I shouldn't.
I crawled into the side of the bed
I knew no one had been--
your grief always a marathon
to the rest of the world's sprint. I ran
my hands along the stitch

of your pillow while you spoke
about the vines covering the windows.
Because the building is historic, the ivy is, too.
I'm not allowed to cut it down, so in the spring
when the leaves grow in, the house is dark
as midnight. But in the winter
when they die, the house is full of light.

Your eyes started closing, as they always had
before mine. Three hours I lay awake, your shoulder
kissing my shoulder. Three hours I stared
at the window, loving you, then turned
toward your ear and whispered that I had to go.

You uncurled from a dream and said, *Okay, Honey.*
And I went to wherever the ivy goes in winter,
and for the same reason.

PHOTOSHOPPING MY SISTER'S MUGSHOT

I crop out the trailer and the splintered remains of the front door.
I crop out your name all over the news.
I crop out the sawed-off shotgun they found hidden in the yard.
I crop out the blood-vacant faces of every soul sold to.
I crop out their family's hunted hearts.

I rotate the image until you are upside down, hanging
from the monkey bars, hollering my name,
Andrea, look what I can do!
I zoom in until there is no lighter beneath the spoon, just ice cream
dripping from your face, and me trying to teach you
how to blow out the candles the day you turned two years old,
your cheeks, pink balloons giggling away gravity.

I give more detail to the background. I pose you
beside our bloodline, our grandfather throwing his liver
through the kitchen window, our grandmother on her knees
sweeping up the glass. I zoom in to the pieces she didn't find.
I find them in the sole of your shoes on your worst day of junior high.

There is a thin line between skewing the truth
and giving a panoramic view. I don't know if I'm widening the lens
or just making an excuse when I say that you were a kid
the first time you used. You wanted blue hair
and a boyfriend, not a conscience

that wouldn't have a good vein left, not an abscess
in the arm you would one day not hold your family with, not me
falling off the wagon of my unforgiveness,
running to the police station, begging them
to replace your photo with the negative,
your dark side in full light,

the filth-hungry scream in your body every time you tried
to get clean, the clinic that told our mother you would die
if she didn't send you back out to the streets
to find the poison, to kill the bugs,
how I'd count your legs when you walked into a room.

How I still do. But that isn't the right exposure.
Because you were also the kindest person I ever knew.
And that in itself has been its own dark room
considering the ugliness is to scale,
considering our family tree

and how there isn't a person who loves you
who isn't dead on the branch.
How loving you less might have been the sweetest gift
I could have given my own life, but how that sweetness
would have rotted god's teeth

when every Christmas morning you woke me at 4 AM,
more excited for me to open my stocking
than you were to open yours.
How do I say that to a judge
and not sound absurd?

How do I say the truth isn't the right filter?
The truth knows nothing
of who you almost were, but I do.
I just click a button. I undo one tiny thing:
        and there you are.

ORLANDO

When the first responders
entered the Pulse nightclub
after the massacre in Orlando,
they walked through the horrific scene
of bodies and called out,
If you are alive, raise your hand.

I was sleeping in a hotel
in the Midwest at the time
but I imagine in that exact moment
my hand twitched in my sleep,
some unconscious part of me aware
that I had a pulse,
that I was alive.

The next day I woke to the news
that an assault rifle had fired
202 bullets through a gay bar
on Latin night in one of the worst
massacres in US history--a massacre
of people who did not leave the dance floor
when they heard gunshots
because they thought
they were just the beats
of the song.

Everyone around me spent
that day grieving and every tear
tasted like dance sweat
drying in the morgue.

Later that night
I was performing for an audience

that had spent two hours in line
waiting to get through bag checks
and metal detectors. On stage
I couldn't keep my hand
from covering

my heart. Kept searching
the club for the fastest route
to every exit. I knew the person
working security was in a text war
and wasn't keeping his eyes
on the door;I knew there was a man
in the fifth row picking at the seams
of a red duffle bag.

Every few seconds
I'd eye the balcony
for the glint
of whatever might aim
to tear the bodies
off the boys holding hands
or the girls with the haircuts short
as my temper when rage
is a decibel I can actually get to
when I'm not just frozen
and grief-sick watching history

not be history, watching
the music not be music, knowing
someone having the best night of her life
shouted, *This is my favorite song,*
and then a drumbeat lifted

a rifle over a bathroom stall
and emptied a magazine

into the kidneys of a grown man
texting, *Mommy, I'm gonna die,*
his handprints in blood
on the walls, reaching

for people
dying in the fetal position,
people covered in their friend's blood,
crying too hard to hide
from their own deaths,
people outside pushing
bandanas into bullet wounds.

It's true
what they say about the gays
being so fashionable--
our ghosts never go
out of style,

even life is like funeral practice:
half of us already dead
to our families before we die,
half of us still on our knees
trying to crawl
into the family photo.

That night on stage I kept remembering
being fifteen at Disney World
wearing my best friend's hoodie
like it was my boyfriend's
class ring.

How many years it took me
to just touch her face,
how many years of praying

my heart could play dead
until the threat was gone,
until the world changed,

until history was history,
but history just keeps coming
for the high, keeps shooting up
bodies, keeps drumming up reasons

to have metal detectors
at poetry readings
where the poems feel
like unanswered calls
to people who claim their god
or their apathy is unwilling
to accept the charges.

Dear god, how broke
do you have to be
to not buy people time
to get out the door
when the song
goes to fucking hell?

When this world, drunk
on hate, decides blood
is wine and drinks its fill
in the only place
they ever thought was safe?
In the only place they thought
they didn't have to hide?

In the only place they were wanted
because of who they loved,
and how they loved
and how they loved,

until someone walked through their bodies
and asked who was still alive
and hardly anyone
put their hand up.

ANDREA/ANDREW

Your name
is a gift

you can return
if it doesn't fit.

GOOD LIGHT

I.
Though I don't remember, I remember my birth
was my first *yes*. Though I was pushed, *yes*.
Though there was screaming, *yes*. Though the light hurt, *yes*.

I wanted the yes to last forever so badly that I told myself:
*We're built like drums. We couldn't make songs
if we had never been hit.* It was a desperate theory.

When they told me god was always watching
I said, *Who wants to worship a diary thief?*
I didn't dare say who wants to worship anyone

who would see everything and just sit there doing nothing
while the devil flossed his teeth with the bow
of my prettiest violin?

They told me the same thing
about Santa always watching and I didn't mind
because he was bringing presents;

god was only bringing life,
which I was told was a sin to return--
even if it didn't fit.

My *yes* never fit into the *no* of this world.
I was just a little girl trying to get rid of the *just* and the *little*,
got rid of the girl instead.

Got rid of my *yes* trying to make a *no* so big
it could go back in time, swallow everything that happened
that should not have happened.

And that's how I lived. That's how I'd been living.
Decades of *no no no no no no no no no.*
And that's okay--an accordion could not make a song

if it never closed.
But then I met you

and I started feeling myself open,
started feeling my yes coming back,

the reverse of being haunted,
like taking a deep breath

and pulling the fog off the glass.
My love, my yes,

do you know how many times a day
my gratitude frames your autograph?

II.
Come see me in the good light.
Come tell me what you tell the truth.
Come trouble me.
Come lightning strike.
Come read out loud what I can't yet pronounce of my own life.
Come wiser than the past.
Come make me make you proud.
Come hope too much.
Come with all your ghosts.
Come clown around when the timing's bad.
Come empty-handed.
Come full of regret.
Come know where it hurts when it doesn't hurt.
Come count to ten with your eyes closed.
Come find me hiding in the place I know you'll look first.

Come promise me the world.
Come trust me to do my best even when I don't.
Come ask me to give you everything I have.
Come knowing I'll give you my word
        that if you fall in the forest when there's no one around
        I'll be there before you land.

Come kind, come searching, come lost.
Come let me find you out.
Come with all your baggage mailed to our house.
Come be everything you are, my love.
Come love this world, come hate it too.
Come undone, come falling apart.
Come every age you have ever been.
Come tantrum in the grocery store.
Come screaming for what's sweet.
Come willing to spill, willing to stain
        the windows of the angry church.
Come nervous brave.

Come tender as the trees
        forgiving the books
            for asking to be made.

Come with all your beauty leaving evidence behind,
        your fingerprints all over the thing that changed my mind,
        that made me better than I was.

Come love, make me better than I was.

Come teach me a kinder way
        to say my own name.

Come share my parachute.
Come let me share your storm.

Come hush the weatherman when he calls it *bad weather*.
Come light as a feather on the bird that stuck around
       to see the snow. I used to drive along the coast of Maine
       searching for the fog.

Come with me to where the sea
       lifts up into the sky just to slow us down.
Come make it count, our finding each other
    like we've found god,
come believing we can heal it all, even everything.

    I know how much the pain of this world weighs
    but I can still tip the scales in light's direction

    whenever I have your name on my tongue.
    Whenever you say love is a ladder

    to our highest selves, I say, *May our falling*
    be the most beautiful climb.

    In the good light, and in the lighting strike,
    come become beside me

    till I find your first silver hair in our tub.
    Till I find your last silver hair in our tub.

ODE TO THE PUBLIC PANIC ATTACK

You find me at the coffee shop,
at the movies, at the grocery store
buying comfort food.

You find me on dates,
which is terrible because on dates
I really try to appear...dateable.

You found me at Disney World,
in line for The Little Mermaid
Slow Moving Clam Ride.

You found me at parties
so often I stopped celebrating
my own birthday.

You found me on an airplane,
then in the arms of the medic
after the plane stopped on the runway

and turned around to let me off.
Don't worry, the medic said,
It's just a panic attack,

as if that would comfort me,
to know I am the enemy,
my body--its own stalker.

Last week, you found me on stage,
and a friend in the crowd said, *That was as awkward*
as watching a goat give birth in the mall.

I think every good artist
makes their audience uncomfortable.
I'd hoped to do that with my politics

and not my body flailing
like the about-to-be-dead girl
in a teenage horror flick,

my own spine curling into the claw
that strips me down to my day of the week panties--
and it is always Doomsday.

Today you found me mid-sentence
while buying tick repellent
at the hardware store.

You chewed the hairs
on the back of my neck
until I couldn't hear the words

panting out of my mouth,
until I wasn't even there
but was in another state

googling *heart palpitations*
and *sudden onset asthma*
and *how many bugs*

are in the human body?
Is it possible to be eaten alive
while someone's eyes

are asking, *Are you OK?*
Are you OK?
No, I'm not OK,

ever. But I am creative,
so when I can't catch my breath
I tell myself, *You're fine,*

that's just your heart
giving your sternum a high five
eighty times a second.

If you've never had a panic attack,
there's a good chance you've been an ass
to someone who has.

JUST RELAX
and *CALM DOWN*
always seem like a helpful things

to scream if oxygen
has never been over your head,
if your body has never become its own corset.

At the restaurant I say, *I have a small bladder,*
because it's less awkward than saying, *I'm going*
to spend most of this outing

in the bathroom stall
falling toward my death
at the speed of darkness

because my parachute
doesn't open
when I leave the house.

I think our culture is beginning to get a tiny bit better
about depression. Often my tears don't go cold
on my cheeks before someone is there,

but we treat panic, anxiety, terror
as the failings of uncourageous minds
who haven't sipped enough chamomile tea

or haven't tattooed Namaste
onto the right part of their windpipe
or haven't picked enough lavender

from their herb gardens
to rub into their
pussy chakra.

A white yogi tells me I can breathe
through the apocalypse in my bloodstream
and I do 6,000 downward dogs

and never stop feeling
the choke of the leash.
I'm done

with the shame. Done
with the cage of self hate. The lie
that this is weakness

when I am certain it is the mightiest proof
of my strength, how hard it is to live
knowing there's a promised jaw

outside my front door
and I still step toward that horror.
Still I say, *Here I am, world!*

Let's make relaxation look like a crime
we'll never get busted for.
Let's hyperventilate like it's 1999.

GENDER IN THE KEY OF LYME DISEASE

I can't carry my own suitcase.
My love carries it for me.
My love is wearing   fever-red   lipstick
and   needle-sharp   stilettos,   smiles
and says, *We're bringing down the patriarchy,*
            hides the heaviness
                of her breath
                        carrying three bags
                            up the stairs.
I fill my backpack
with crumpled paper
so it looks like I can carry   heavy things.
I tell myself I couldn't lift my backpack
        if my heart was in it.
Tell myself my hero died
of the same disease and didn't
lose a battle with anything, was still
my hero.   My hero used a new pronoun in the eulogy.
I'm always thinking about the gender   of dying,
and the gender of surviving.   I hear animals
in the wild won't reproduce
with animals they know are sick.   I go wild
worrying my love is lying when she says she loves me.
        How attractive can a person be in an MRI machine?
I never let her pay for anything—
my wallet the only thing   not too thin.
I'd be fucked up over thinking   a wallet masculine
if I had the energy.   I'd be fucked up
over watching my feminism atrophy.
My doctor tells me the immune system
is the boundary system of the body, tells me
my boundaries aren't working now
            like they didn't work way back then.

I think, *My fault*   *I'm sick,*   *probably asked for it.*
I wonder if I'd look more alive
if I wore my love's makeup.
I try it on when she's not home, then get terrified
my eyelashes are longer than my lifelines.
Lately my lifelines   won't stop   pouring
down my cheeks. My love finds me
on the bathroom floor, kisses them
onto her lips so when she speaks
I can see   there's life in me.   She talks me down
to our tandem bike that I ride on the back of
with my feet up, summer running
its fingers through my hair, but secretly
          my favorite season   is flu season.
                    The season of proof   that I'm tough
          as Christ   forgiving   the nails.
The season everyone I love becomes
a raging customer at the complaint counter of life,
like their birth certificates were warranties,
their bodies promised technology
guaranteeing protection from all viruses.
They break down, Nyquil drunk
and say, *I haven't been able*
to exercise in three days.
          The last time I got the flu   it took me three days
to notice.   I thought the pain   was just the pain.
          I thought the Charley horse bucking
through my body   was just another day
I couldn't tame.
When my love   took my temperature
and it read 103   I pranced   around the house,
the happiest   she'd seen me in two years—
high on the news that I had something
that would go away.   Good god,
          there isn't a healthy body in the world

that is stronger than a sick person's spirit.
Thirty times last month I thought, *I can't do this another day.*
Thirty times last month I did it another day.　　　I lived
with the hurt　　burrowing into my bloodstream,
and still wanted more time　　　more than I wanted
the tweezers　　to tear the fucking ticks
　　　from the fucking clock.
I wanted more time more than I wanted heaven
to make the pain to stop.　　　I don't know
the gender of living. I think maybe it's just admitting
　　　how badly　　I want my mother
　　　　　to see me　　and comment on the pink
in my cheeks. Maybe it's coming out of the closet
with all of it, knowing　　　even when the truth isn't hopeful
the telling of it is.　　　Truth is—I've had nothing　　but paper
in my backpack since 2003. You wouldn't believe
how much the hiding
has weighed.

DIAGNOSIS

I suffer
from unrequited self love.
I love myself, but I don't
love myself
back.

BOOMERANG VALENTINE

I'm sitting on my friend's couch several months
into being intentionally single and celibate
for the first time since I was twenty years old,

twenty years old, when I believed sex
had to involve a dude and the word *screw*.
I'm telling my friend about the psychic

who said I'm gonna meet the love of my life
by the end of January. It's January 10th
and I am so far from ready

for Cupid, that naked little shit,
to fire anything sharp my way,
so far from ready to be the kind of unhinged

only love makes me. My friend musters every bit
of New Age jargon she can fit onto her tongue and says, *What if
you are the love of your life?* I think, *Oh my god, I hope*

that's not true,
because I am absolutely
not my type.

But let's say for a moment I am.
Let's say I am my dream girl-

ish boy, and I'm standing on my front porch
ringing my own doorbell waiting for me to answer

so I can hand myself a mason jar full of water lilies
I have rescued from a millionaire's Monet.

Let's say I am so charmed by the radiance
of my own anarchy, I invite myself in

for tea, and when I'm not looking, I sneak
the steam from the kettle into my pocket

so the next time I'm missing the coast of Maine
I can gift myself the fog.

Let's say I'm not just running my mouth
around an old cliché that says we gotta love ourselves.

We don't. I know I could
keep getting down on myself

until I'm tucked in my grave, looking up at my name
carved in stone, wondering why I never knew

I'd been cast for the lead in my own life.
When it comes to love the only thing I'm certain of is:

you are the best thing
that has ever happened to you.

Whoever you are. You're a quitter? Great.
There's plenty worth quitting.

A sore loser? Who isn't?
Got no discipline? Maybe discipline is for bodybuilders

and closeted gay monks.
Picture a magician

so attached to being perfect
he cuts off his own legs to pull off the trick.

Picture the 738 selfies I deleted
before I took one I was willing to show to the world.

Picture me wishing I could get all of them back—
my so-called flaws stacked like baseball cards

I know will be worth something someday,
like compassion, like tenderness,

like my capacity to think myself a catch just because
I have never seen a chandelier I didn't want to swing from.

On days I have a hard time keeping warm
in my own weather, I imagine what the flower wanted to say

to the first human trying to name half its petals love-me-nots:
No, that is not how anything grows.

Of all the violence I have known in my life
I have never known violence

like the violence I have spoken to myself,
and I have seen almost everyone around me

hold that same belt to their own back,
an ambush of every way we've decided we're not enough,

then looking for someone outside of ourselves
to clean that treason up.

If I were to ask myself out
of that cycle, I might say, *Listen,*

I am still going through a growth spurt.
I am still yet to get my worst tattoo. I am still trying

to get rid of my mirror face. I am still learning
to look myself dead in the eye.

I know Facebook is a lousy mortician
desperately trying to make us all look more alive.

I know there are things I haven't survived.
I know there are people in this world

who have been through hell with me.
I don't ever want to take that lightly,

but I want the heavy to anchor me brave, anchor me
loving, anchor me in something that will hold me

to my word when I tell Cupid I intend to keep walking out
to the tip of his arrow, to bend it back toward myself,

to aim for my goodness until the muscle in my chest tears
from the stretch of becoming what I came here to be: a lover

of whatever got covered up by the airbrush,
the truth of me, that beauty of a beast

chewing through the leash
until I got a mason jar full of water lilies

and a kettle full of sea, and my whole life
is a boomerang valentine

coming right back at me.

THANKSTAKING

Before the animal sanctuary
where I hugged a turkey, feathered angel
nuzzling under my chin, before I knew
turkeys love to be hugged, before I was
old enough to volunteer to serve
meals at the church, before I heard
the preacher's wife scold a man
without a home for not being grateful enough,
before I was queer enough to notice
my name left out of a prayer,
before I got the scoop on what really happened
at Plymouth Rock, before I learned the word
genocide, before I knew enough
to be devastated that I'd once asked my friend
how her family celebrated Thanksgiving
on the reservation, before we marched
the streets closed, before I'd held hands
with a crying 5-year-old running from riot cops
throwing tear gas, before we shut down
the parade anyway carrying signs
that said *Thankstaking*, it was my favorite holiday—
I cut paper bags into pilgrim clothes
and put on Mayflower living rooms shows,
I grabbed the wishbone with both hands
and won the wish every year, I ate potatoes,
my favorite, from morning until midnight—
I don't remember another day
my family was so happy;
my mother could still stand
on her head back then,
and I'd laugh the stuffing out of my nose,
her feet shooting toward the sky like a toy arrow,
her face red as beet—I hated beets and I never had

to eat them on Thanksgiving—*it was the best day,*
I was thinking last summer, roasting marshmallows
with my parents in the backyard of my home,
the flames like arms reaching to beckon us closer
to each other, when my mother, casually,
like it was nothing, said her father—who I knew
she'd loved more than life, who I knew had died
when she was still a kid—had died on Thanksgiving,
a fact I'd never known all those years,
what I'd called *the best day* had been the anniversary
of her very worst day, my god, I thought,
how many times did she sneak into her bedroom
to take his photo out of the drawer, how many times
did she try to catch her reflection in the window
to make sure her mascara wasn't bleeding
down her cheeks, have I ever since and will I ever again
know a generosity so wide as her smile
all those years, how wildly she clapped
for my joy, the whole slaughter of a day,
a day she gave to me—her tiny pilgrim
giddy with having no idea what I had
to be grateful for.

AMERICA WAKES ME IN THE MIDDLE OF THE NIGHT

tells me
she had a bad dream
one where the bootstraps
hung families from trees

one where the morgue
pinned flowers
on prom suits

one where the casket
was a full stomach
growling for more

in the dream
america elected a president
who told the truth

didn't bother
wearing a sheet

knew his shoes
would be recognized
on wall street anyway

in the dream
america was not
who she thought she was

forgot
how to pronounce
her own name—Dakota,
Passamaquoddy,
Shoshoni, Cherokee

in the dream
all the polls said hate
was history

hate was an animal
gone extinct

in the dream
no one polled
the truth

no one polled
its teeth

no one polled
how easily
the nightstick swung
in broad daylight

no one polled
the auction
of zimmerman's gun

no one polled
the massacre
in the nightclub

no one polled
the "good" nazis

no one polled
what the wall
would keep in

the pipeline
through the prayer

pence
quoting Dr. King

the trump tower
replacing the statue
of liberty

in the dream
the worst sentence
anyone could get
was life

in the dream
the thorn was Christ

in the dream
america drank
who she killed
in church

trusted the comfortable
would keep
holding their tongues
like whips

worshipped
the red flag

fought god
for the rights
to the apocalypse

WHITE FEMINISM [NOUN]

1.   A racism that claims
it is at least better
than no feminism at all,
like at least Hitler
was a vegetarian,
like we could actually
get comfortable
being the uneaten animal
in the lap of the man
making lampshades
out of human skin.

THE DAY YOU DIED BECAUSE YOU WANTED TO

i tied my wisdom tooth to a doorknob
and pulled it loose. take everything
i think i know. every answer
is a grave. the questions are the warm rain
i walk through now to find my way
to god, and my only god is faith
that there is comfort here,
that who is hurting will hurt less
than they did before. what else
are all these coins and all these wells for
if not to wish the grief asleep
in the lap of someone's else's grief,
till grief comes not knowing
if it will come again. your sister
thought the hearse was a limousine
until she asked where it was going,
and then she knew for sure.
that's what a word like *heaven* will do.
but heaven wasn't what you were aiming for.
you didn't think the other side would be better.
you thought the other side would be nothing at all.
imagine choosing nothing at all. imagine
something hurting that bad.
i didn't still have the ring you gave me.
i crushed it with a rock to see
how much you loved me. i love you
to pieces too. and love should have been enough,
someone without a heart might say. it hurts me
in my head now. how you knew the water
wasn't deep enough to dive into.
but i don't let anyone say it was a shallow thing
you did. i knew it was your entire body

finally pointing, saying here, here is where the pain is.
i can crush a can with the heel of my shoe.
i can drive by your mother's house
if i want to, but i don't want to. she was there
when you bought the ring. she knew
how long you'd been saving. me,
i didn't save anything. but you don't lose a person
like a set of keys because you don't find them again
and you can still get to where you're going. resilience
itself is an awful thing to grieve.
who with a heart can stomach
how much they can stomach?
all your blood in the water
and i could still wade through,
and i will again and i will again
and i will again with everyone i lose.
what i want most is to live
the rest of my life desperately
wanting to live it. i want to give that to you.
i want it to find you in the nothing at all.
i want it to be something.
when i say i want to make something of my life—
that's what i mean.

TINCTURE

Imagine, when a human dies, the soul misses the body, actually grieves the loss of its hands and all they could hold. Misses the throat closing shy reading out loud on the first day of school. Imagine the soul misses the stubbed toe, the loose tooth, the funny bone. The soul still asks, *Why does the funny bone do that? It's just weird.* Imagine the soul misses the thirsty garden cheeks watered by grief. Misses how the body could sleep through a dream. What else can sleep through a dream? What else can laugh? What else can wrinkle the smile's autograph? Imagine the soul misses each falling eyelash waiting to be a wish. Misses the wrist screaming away the blade. The soul misses the lisp, the stutter, the limp. The soul misses the holy bruise blue from that army of blood rushing to the wound's side. When a human dies, the soul searches the universe for something blushing, something shaking in the cold, something that scars, sweeps the universe for patience worn thin, the last nerve fighting for its life, the voice box aching to be heard. The soul misses the way the body would hold another body and not be two bodies but one pleading god doubled in grace. The soul misses how the mind told the body, *You have fallen from grace.* And the body said, *Erase every scripture that doesn't have a pulse. There isn't a single page in the bible that can wince, that can clumsy, that can freckle, that can hunger.* Imagine the soul misses hunger, emptiness, rage, the fist that was never taught to curl—curled, the teeth that were never taught to clench—clenched, the body that was never taught to make love—made love like a hungry ghost digging its way out of the grave. The soul misses the unforever of old age, the skin that no longer fits. The soul misses every single day the body was sick, the *now* it forced, the *here* it built from the fever. Fever is how the body prays, how it burns and begs for another average day. The soul misses the legs creaking up the stairs, misses the fear that climbed up the vocal cords to curse the wheelchair. The soul misses what the body could not let go—what else could hold on that tightly to everything? What else could see hear the chain of a swing set and fall to its knees? What else could touch a screen door and taste lemonade? What else could come back from a war and not come back? But still try to live? Still try to lullaby? When a human dies the soul moves through the universe trying to describe how a body trembles when it's lost, softens when it's safe, how a wound would heal given nothing but time. Do you understand? Nothing in space can imagine it. No comet, no nebula, no ray of light can fathom the landscape of awe, the heat of shame. The fingertips pulling the first gray hair and throwing it away. *I can't imagine it,* the stars say. *Tell us again about goosebumps. Tell us again about pain.*

AWESTRUCK [VERB]

1. to quit
    building bomb shelters
    to keep the universe
    from blowing your mind.

RADIO

turning the dial of the radio in my car
running through the rain in a dress

slicing avocados in my kitchen
sleeping in the guest room of my house

biting her lip
at my bedroom door

sweet as a tourist at a slot machine
hungry as a last bet

putting down my pick-up lines
picking her teeth with the hook

flipping off the mistletoe
slipping her hand down my jeans on the bus

trimming her fingernails on my mother's couch
winking then blowing me a kiss

offering me an apple daring me
to demand the orchard insisting i come

from her rib
burning through the sugarcoat

burning out my clutch
topless in my car

telling me to keep my eyes on the road
her knuckles between my teeth

her law on my side
pulling me over to teach me

the respectable way
to tear up a permission slip

dropping it like rose petals on her way up the stairs
taking the mirror off the bedroom wall

whispering *don't you want something*
you'd be ashamed to witness

breaking my fever with the slide of her hips
kicking the legs out from under my doubt

fighting for our honor swinging for the picket fence
naked in the dugout

waking me from a nightmare
hanging my past like a sail

wiping the sweat from my forehead
whispering *we can go anywhere*

holding my hand on the plane
wearing my hoodie to the store

breaking up a bar fight
by calling my name

running her fingers through my hair
in a restaurant in the midwest

walking through the cemetery in my hometown
fixing the flowers on a stranger's grave

carrying our dog to the vet
holding the ladder while i hang our wreath

calling from our porch to come look at the sky
calling from our bedroom to come zip up her dress

asking for my number every time we kiss
looking up from her book to say *listen to this line*

stopping me from carving our initials into a tree
whispering *everything that grows already knows who we are*

in her underwear eating ice cream on our roof
in her nightgown filling a bird feeder in our backyard

in nothing but our sweat on the living room floor
turning the dial of our radio

saying *baby listen*
you haven't heard this song before

"WHAT DO YOU THINK ABOUT THIS WEATHER?"

Well—I think it's untrue that no two snowflakes are the same. I think the snowflakes are just holding their hands in different positions— high-fives, and peace signs, and hitchhiker thumbs, and middle finger *fuck yous*. Every winter I try to catch as many *fuck yous* on my tongue as I can. It's the feminist in me. I also think we make way too many snowmen and too few snowwomen. If I'd seen more snowwomen growing up I might have learned how to flood the city every time someone told me to disappear. I might have learned how to load my rocky smile into a slingshot whenever a dude suggested smiling was something I should do. *You're right, man! Here ya go—pew!* Where I come from it got so cold we made bonfires in the middle of the lake. There'd be this huge fire and we'd be skating around the truth that all of us, like the ice, would one day have to hold that much—the impossible even. My father said not to worry. He said, *heat rises*. But heat rises for the same reason people rise—because they have to. I think the heat would like to rest sometime, don't you? My mother used to knit my mittens too big so they'd still fit me when I grew. I wore them and looked like who I wasn't yet. I feel that sometimes when I'm writing poems—like they don't yet fit. Do you ever feel like the best of you is something you're still hoping to grow into? I don't consider myself a cold person but there's that wind-chill factor. I think I got mine from my grandma. She'd sit in church and curse like a witch. Do you know witch-hunts happened more commonly in cold weather because people looked for scapegoats to blame for hardship? I know exactly who I've burned for my own failed crop. I used to fall too fast in love a lot. I used to make diamonds out of icicles and promise they would last. My father taught me how to make ice cream out of snow by adding milk and maple syrup. I've eaten more snow than anyone I know. I say that on a first date now. I say, *The storm is in me.* I say, *Promise you'll leave me if your heating bill goes up.* When my grandma died I went home and made a snow angel on her grave, and then I made another so she wouldn't be alone.

I heard loneliness resonates in the same part of the brain as physical pain. One year before Christmas I visited a men's prison, and when I was leaving the snow started falling on the barbed wire fence and I looked back to see if there were faces watching it from the windows, but there were no windows. That was the same year 8,962 people in North Dakota laid down on their backs and made snow angels at the same time. If I had been there I know I would have proposed to whoever was beside me, some angel with a smile all her own and the good sense to say, *I don't know. Maybe.* When my father was a kid he'd walk his sled to the top of the city in a snowstorm and his friends would stand at each intersection at every block below and my father would come flying down and his friends would stop traffic and holler, *Go, go, go!* But enough about me—what do you think about the weather? Do igloos blow your mind? Have you ever gotten your tongue stuck to something cold? Have you forgiven her yet?

DEAR TINDER,

I know it's not your fault
she lied to me, but you did
make it so easy for her

to swipe the sweetness
off my face.

When she finally told me,
I made her pretty stranger's photo
the screensaver on my phone.

That's how twisted I am,
even after all the therapy,

still not right in the head,
still a lefty, playing
my instruments upside down.

But I know what the devil's
favorite music is—the sound of responsibility

being thrown in every direction
but home. I hear almost every argument
is a race for the victim spot.

I've historically been first
to cross that line.

But blame is its own hell
so I've been working my ash off.
Counting how many times

I've been cheated on and seeing how much
of that I own—a decade crying

about being lied to by a woman
who was wearing a wedding ring
the first time she had her hand inside of me.

Only I know how broke I got
buying into the theory

that my life is something that happens
to me, that we are more holy
the more hurt we are.

I know what that thought has taken
from my life. What I stole

from myself opening my chest
like a wound. Her lie was just a speck of sand
in the hourglass of truth.

A house we built
with both our hands.

AMERICA, RELOADING

Mostly because of dying stars,
scientists say space smells like barbecue
and gunpowder. Which is to say
space smells like the United States—

a holiday where we celebrate the independence
of machine guns, how anyone can buy
a cemetery at a sporting goods store
on their 18th birthday

and open carry it to an elementary school
where children are learning tears
don't fall in space. Weightless, without
gravity, they never leave the eye.

Is that what happens to the NRA?
they ask after they've watched the bodies
of half their class use every red crayon
in the universe to scream goodbye.

> *Do the NRA's tears not drop*
> *because they're astronauts?*

How does a parent tell a 6-year-old
that gun sales spike every time
our right to bear massacres
makes a coroner faint,

> makes a mortician say, *I can't,*
> *my god, I can't.*

But we can, can't we, America?
Each election don't we say we *can*

stomach the boy loading a black hole
into his backpack and unloading it

in the high school hallway
on Valentine's day. It would take
light years to count how many times
the terrified texted *I LOVE YOU,*

I LOVE YOU, I LOVE YOU
in Parkland, Florida
while the NRA kept crying
      in space.

My friend, a second grade teacher,
is instructed to practice hiding her children
in the closet. Twenty-three 7-year-olds
huddle holding their breath.

     Holding your breath in space
       is the fastest way to die.

The lungs explode in that vacuum
almost as quickly as an AR-15
can make blood-dust
of a closet door.

Of the twenty children murdered at Sandy Hook,
not one of them needed an ambulance.
That's how dead they were.
That's how well the Second Amendment works.

Because there is no air, it is silent in space.
But not as silent as the Christians
on the Senate floor while twenty more families
are asked if they'd like to talk

to a priest. Christ could tear the nails
from his hands and scrape them down
a shrapnel-battered chalkboard
and they'd still be praying for their bank accounts.

After Columbine, parents were notified
about their children in tiny conference rooms.
One family said, *We could hear the family before us
screaming, and we knew we were next.*

Now loved ones check Facebook
to see who is dead. A mother's status is, *I CAN'T
REACH MY DAUGHTER. I CAN'T REACH
MY DAUGHTER.* Decades after her child is slaughtered

in the cafeteria
that thought will still be
tearing her from her bed—*I CAN'T
REACH MY DAUGHTER—*

The footprints left by astronauts
on the moon are permanent.
They will never ever go away
like the grief of a father

identifying his son by his shoes
because the rest of his son's body
was out-lobbied by the NRA, by suits
whispering into the ears of Washington—

this is what we mean
by freedom and justice, the names
of our cities becoming synonymous
with babies being buried

like seeds in the greed gardens of the wealthy.
But you should know your teacher
was a hero, we say. *Her body was found*
bunkering a group of your friends.

And that's as happy as the ending gets
right now. The heroes almost always dead.
The flag at half mass grave.
Children huddled

in basements, trying to tear off their ears
on the Fourth of July because the fireworks
sound like the day everyone died crying,
died with gravity pouring

their next 80 birthdays from their eyes,
while America reloaded,
       and moved on
            to the next.

BLACK AND WHITE ANGEL

After six months awaiting sentencing in the county jail,
after the tremors slept and each abscess walked backward
until it was only a dot on the pink horizon of her open arms,
my sister's court date was scheduled for Halloween.

During their final visit, her daughter
explained her costume, a black and white angel,
which is an angel not entirely innocent.
Not every little girl wants to grow up
to be her mother, but my niece does.

In the visitation room, the clock on the wall doubled in size
with each passing minute. My sister told stories
about how she'd made eye shadow
from a crushed colored pencil, her lunch made her lip gloss and blush.
Sober now, I knew the eternity of meals she would trade
to be beautiful for her daughter,

who was laughing as often as she could to lift the heaviness
in her mother's chest, her grief a joke
she kept pretending to understand,
her laughter a holy lie
she should have been too young
to know how to tell.

During the visit, my niece only broke once,
and only when the guard rattled his keys and rushed her
to finish hugging her mother, the nightstick of his voice cracking
over their bleeding goodbye. I restrained my fist in my pocket
but wanted to knock him back

to his own mother's arms,
where he might grow into a man

without a uniform over his chest.
My sister isn't innocent
but neither is the system

that denies the disease of addiction.
I know rabies when I see it. I know who she was
before she was bit--thirteen and still getting homesick
at sleepovers, unable to close her eyes without the warm milk
of our mother's smile poured into the night's cup.

After several months inside,
when she had asked me to mail her a book
on dreams, I sent it, wanting her to be able to read herself
with as much tenderness as the letters
that might arrive to her cell in a child's penmanship.

I knew how desperately she wanted her daughter
to unknow the price of stamps, to one day be able
to walk into the kitchen and ask her what a tampon is.
The morning of her sentencing, I prayed in the shower,
begged anybody's god to let her be the one

to someday make the curfew that pissed her daughter off.
Prayed my niece would get the chance to hate her mother
like every other teenager hates her mother, for the unforgivable crime
of not giving enough space, or for saying, I love you, too loudly
in front of a group of cute boys.

As I walked into the courtroom, I kept picturing
my niece sitting at her elementary school desk.
I remembered how they'd sent home a note
saying no one was to wear a costume to class on Halloween.
But what choice did she have

but to wear the mask of a little girl
when in real life she too was being tried as an adult?

Finding out how many lines would be left for her mother
to draw on the doorframe—or if there would be any lines
left at all. When she too was waiting to find out

how many years she would serve before being free?
When the judge walked in and we were all asked
to rise, I heard her fall
to the floor of her classroom
to crush a colored pencil into powder.

Right before the verdict was read, I heard her again,
telling another holy lie in the lunchroom
about why she could not eat the strawberries on her plate,
why she could not swallow what might be the only thing left
of her mother's face.

DEPRESSION [VERB]

1. to put on
    your best outfit
    and feel
    like you're dressing
    a wound.

BABY TEETH IN A LANDFILL

Goddammit, I miss believing in everything.
Who wants a universe where things are what they are?

The sun doesn't actually rise, the scientist says.
The earth is just rotating on its axis.

Your baby teeth are in a landfill
next to your brother's shitty diapers.

Santa Claus loves the rich
way more than the poor.

The other day I watched a pickup truck swerve
to hit a squirrel.

Last month my favorite musician quit music
because the crowd requested his most famous song.

Why am I here with all these rocks
in Virginia Woolf's pocket?

When are the shooting stars gonna aim
for that orange guy's head? Can I get arrested

for saying that? Does he identify
as *Orange Guy*? Good thing I'm here

googling *how to make prison mascara*
for my baby sister.

I used to plant flowers
in New Orleans.

One day my molar crumbled out of my mouth
and I said, *Look how much sweetness I have known!*

Nobody fingerpaints anymore.
Nobody makes crowns out of paper bags.

Where did the days of playing saxophone in the pep band
during halftime of my own basketball games go?

What happened to sweating all over
the keys, then running back to the court

where every shitty call
was still somebody whistling at me?

What happened?
I used to be somebody

who smoked opium by accident,
who huffed gasoline and sang

Mariah Carey to the seagulls, who wrapped
a boa constrictor around my neck

just for the photo.
Once I got proposed to

just hours after leaving the psych ward.
Where did the romance go?

I think I might be trapped
in a miserable person's body.

There is a world in which all the bad things
that happened didn't really happen

and this
is not that world.

This is a life without sunrise.
This is the shitty earth on its shitty axis.

This is the best advice for insomnia
anyone has ever given me: *TRY TO STAY AWAKE.*

So I try to hate this world.
And then I wait...

BAD AT LOVE

I bought a typewriter when we said goodbye,
hoping to make a life I couldn't erase so easily
the next time. But the next time

I just burned the page. It wasn't her.
It was me, hating what I was
wearing whenever I was wearing my heart

on my sleeve, kept changing my outfit
into something made for the cold.
Understanding why we're bad at love

doesn't necessarily make us good at it.
I wasn't good at it even though I knew
I couldn't take a compliment

without feeling like a thief,
couldn't believe anything past the first page of me
was worth the read. It was a lie

when I said I couldn't take the long distance.
It was that I didn't want to drive
anything but a getaway car—

mistook love for the scene of a crime.
You'd touch me and I'd collect the fingerprints
for proof that the past would never run itself dry,

that love would always be watering a wound,
that pain would never be a dead thing
I could pull up by its roots.

All that time in the garden
of my shame growing roses
for your rose-colored glasses

so you would never see the color leave my face,
never see me scared, never call me
prey. I'd show my teeth and tell you

I was just hungry for the truth. And I was
hungry for the truth. I just couldn't keep it down.
Some people fall out of love.

I jump
to feel the safety
of the parachute.

HURT THE FLY

Your therapist asks what you're
feeling and you say you're sick of
talking about the symptoms. There's
an arrow through your sternum and
you're being asked how it feels, how
you're planning to work with the
arrow there, how you're planning to
breathe in a crowded room. You
don't want to talk anymore about
where to hide the blades in the
house when the arrow gets you
desperate for a pain only you
control. You just want the arrow out.
You want to grab the past and tear it
from your body even if it takes your
organs with it. There are lists for
new organs. No lists for new pasts.
A few years ago a friend asked if
you'd ever had a childhood. You
said, *No*—but that wasn't right.
What you haven't had is an
adulthood. The wound still your
mouth. The tantrum still your world.
Nothing ever louder in your head
than the thought, *I'm way too young
for this.* How little you were when
you started wanting your mother to
love you

less—so it wouldn't kill her to know
you'd been hurt. You still can't
stomach telling the truth without
some bungee in the noose. Without
saying the worst thing that ever
happened to you was not the worst
thing that ever happened to you.
Hating yourself for it was. Your
therapist says the shame is trying to
take care of you. Says you blame
yourself so you can believe the
world is a safe place, or would be if
only you had done things differently.

It's kind of sweet actually,
what you've given to believe
   in the goodness of the world—
your own good name,
         your own good light,
your own wise and grown life,
         all traded for a galaxy
         that wouldn't hurt
         a fly.

FIRST DATE

I am twenty one
and newly queer,
my hair still permed
and ponytailed
with a scrunchie.
I have a huge crush
on an older butch woman
who rides a motorcycle,
smokes cigars and drinks
non-alcoholic beer
like she has run
pants down
from the fist
of some beautiful
woman's husband
just the right
amount of times.
Because I'm young
and fairly assuming,
and because I've just read
Stone Butch Blues,
I assume if I sleep
with a butch woman
she's going to want to
get up into my groove--
if you know what I mean.
And because I have
very little experience
with someone
getting up into my groove,
I decide I should first
practice going up there
alone. But being too shy

to walk into a sex shop
to buy a dildo,
I find myself
one summer afternoon
at a church yard sale
paying a church lady
twenty-five cents
for a toy snake.
I take the snake home,
put a condom on it
for safety's sake
and also because
I don't want to see
its eyes,
and I get up
into my groove
for the first time.
I know this
is our first date
and that's a lot
to share over nachos,
but I'd ideally tell you
everything about me,
preferably before dessert.
And by everything,
I mean every
reptilian urge,
or more specifically
every time I have ever
had the devil inside me—
that's a metaphor.
I'm not still talking
about the snake.

NO FILTER

I am a living reaction to my hurt,
a beginner cowboy trying to lasso
my traumas into the stable.
I am hardly ever stable.
Last week I busted my knuckle
on the steering wheel
because I believed for a moment
I'd made a wrong turn
when I became who I am.
I'd go into detail but it will hurt too much.
I hurt too much to be a saint.
Most of us do. My therapist
wants me to join a boxing gym
so to not break my skeleton
on what gets me to where I need to go,
so to not break that unspoken promise we all make
to be in real life whoever we are on Instagram.
On Instagram I am a cartwheel on the beach,
a typewriter collection, a pink umbrella
beneath a stormless sky, a snow angel
on my grandmother's grave.
On Instagram I breathe
and a dandelion seed learns how to fly.
On Instagram I am never a weed,
never what kills the garden, never cold
as the frost, never punching the steering wheel
and icing my knuckles in a gas station parking lot.
But please, don't let me be
the kind of person whose crimes get revealed
after I die. May it all be written while I'm still alive,
even this: In the sixth grade, I left a note in a locker
that I still worry made a girl rethink her beauty
for the rest of her life.

ALL THE GOOD IN YOU

When all the good in you
starts arguing with all the bad in you
about who you really are,
never let the bad in you
make the better case.

GIVE HER

If I hadn't sold it for its gold,
I would give her the class ring I wore
when I was still a girl
and taking good care of my cuticles.

If it hadn't burned in a fire,
I'd give her the Valentine
from my first kiss—
the bully who grew up
to become a preacher.

If I knew where to find it
I'd give her the time capsule I buried
to open in a million years,
I'd shimmy it out of the earth,

and say, *Here, I made this for you
when I was seven.* Inside: a lock
of my dog's hair from before
he went to live on a farm

for biting the face off a man
who looked at me wrong.
If the tooth fairy hadn't come
any of those times, I'd give her my smile

and say, *You're the reason why I'm gay,*
and I mean that the old fashioned way
as in happy, but also
the other way, too.

I would give her my name,
but I'd rather have hers

so when the telemarketers call
and say, *With whom am I speaking?*

I could say it aloud, the name
I was born with, but didn't know
until the night I wiped the sweat off her arms
on a dance floor in Oakland,

then licked her salt off the length of my hand.
Do you understand how sick a person gets
licking their hands in a nightclub?
I didn't leave the bathroom for seven days,

which is to say I want to give her my time,
my decades even. Don't tell me to be less dramatic.
Of course I've loved before, but I didn't
give it my all. Mostly I gave up.

She asks me what makes this different.
Why I want to give it a whirl the size of a tornado?
Why I want to give it a go at every red light?
I just know she makes me feel

like I could win the lottery
with a parking ticket. I see her
lipstick on a coffee cup
and feel like I have never known a bruise.

I say, *I want to give it my best,*
and I want my best to be incredible
because people take me serious,
but I know I'm a joke

she will always get,
her laughter so holy, the hecklers

tell me I'm coming up short and I think, great,
now I can win the limbo contest.

I want to give her all my trophies
from the county fair
where I won the potato sack race
and the poetry slam

where I was the runner-up behind a man
who wrote a love poem
about pudding
(that would be the sweetest gift).

When she's down I want to give her my best
pick-up lines. *What's your sign?*
My sign has historically been STOP
but since meeting you I've changed it

to MERGE.
Darling, when I gave you my heart,
I gave my life, my word
that it would not be the same heart

I had given before.
I put in, like, a hundred more doors
and a record player from a real record store
and I put in a skylight that is all yours

that day you picked me up and carried me
through that airport
like my goodbye had no weight.
My goodbye has no weight.

Right now you are sleeping beside me
making a face you would not want

to know you're making. Call it the opposite
of your mirror face. Call it me bringing home the gold.

Call our bed sheets what was sewn
from the ribbon at the end of a race.
I don't want to be anywhere but here
whispering all your nicknames

from every hiding place until I give myself away:
Hey Galaxy, Hey Lord of the Butterflies, Hey Pudding,
Hey Windchime, Hey Grief Thief,
Hey Center-Folded Love Note, Hey Holy Spooner,

Hey Spaceship Believer, Hey Adorable Sneezer,
Hey Rose Water, Hey Favorite Sleepover,
Hey Perfect S'more, Hey LifeBoat, Hey Lifeboat,
I'm yours.

SAID THE WISHING WELL

It has been years
since anyone has come
for water,
but there is still a bucket here
and it is always full.
Thirst is such a simple thing
to heal. The first time a coin fell
I thought it was a gift,
a strange gift,
a small piece of copper
carved with the face
of a sad man.
Then I heard the boy
praying in the wrong direction.
Why do they so often laugh
when they cry? Who taught them
to be ashamed of needing
more than water?
I never know their names.
People, in their wanting,
are only what they are
to another: a sister, an enemy,
a mother who blames herself
for everything but still believes in god.
It is not what I wanted,
even in my loneliness, to be rich
with what they long for, to shine
with what they are sure they need,
to watch their soft bodies wilt
from not drinking
what has always
been here.

DEAR TRUMP VOTER,

The Nazis built gas chambers, in part, to save the humanity of the firing squad. Some general looked into the eyes of his men firing into the screams of children, of pregnant women bending their own heads to swallow the bullets aimed at the kick in their bellies, and the general thought, "If we keep forcing these men to kill like this, what is human in them will die. Their guilt will be ungovernable." The Holocaust needed its killers to believe they were not the killers. As disgusting as it sounds, the gas chamber was a product of recognizing human conscience. Auschwitz murdered 6,000 people a day, and the murderer was Zyclon B, hydrogen cyanide, nothing human in that name, nobody's father bursting the lungs of millions clawing the concrete for god. But the gas chamber was not a Nazi invention. It is American as apple pie to want to stretch the distance between the killer and the crime, to say you are not responsible for the child searching the smoke in the air for the shape of her mother's face. It was an American invention: the "I wasn't there," the "Don't blame me," the "I didn't see it happen," the "I'm not racist but—." The first gas chamber was built in the Nevada desert on the stolen land of the Washoe people to murder a Chinese man without a white person's conscience having to carry the shame of his kill home. I know you take issue with me comparing Trump to Hitler. One, a failed painter who blamed the Jewish people for the beauty his heart was too ugly to make. The other, a con artist with enough failed humanity to eye our dying planet and focus on Miss America's weight. I wish I didn't know what men who feel inadequate have in common, what they believe they are owed: the first blood of our bodies or—your vote. Your vote for a man who said he'd date his daughter if she wasn't already his. Your vote for man who is guaranteeing every woman a jury of her rapist's peers. Your vote for man who is filling the American pie with the apples in the throats of girls in the "wrong" restrooms. Your vote for a man who has bet on people's lives that he can keep Muslim protests against ISIS out of the news. Your vote for a man promising to build a wall between the thirst and the river. A firing squad is a firing squad. In the history of the US it was never more clear that a vote would be a bullet. There is no distance between you and the blood. The truth will not give an inch to the lie of innocence, to the governable denial of anyone who continues to aim for the head while calling it making something great again.

UNTIL WE ACT

The man asks what I think
the US should be doing about Syria
and I wonder how to answer that
from here—where the planes
overhead mean tropical vacations,
where looking up is what we do
to feel hopeful,

not what we do to decide
when to tell our children
to run from the air,
to hide the sunrise of their lungs.

My mother never had to teach me
that to breathe is to die, so I imagine

her hand covering my mouth
in the dark of our basement,
tasting her palm salted
with terror. I imagine

because to not imagine
is its own missile, its own gas,
its own horrid war.

I imagine because Syria is 6,677 miles away
but would still be called our neighbor
if her children were as white as our eyes.

I know the white of the eye
is the part that does not see.

The closest I might ever come to war
is the turning of my head.
Apathy is intimate, like singing a lullaby

to a grenade,
then drinking yourself to sleep
while it sneaks out the window
to explode a boy. I heard

there is a town outside of Damascus,
years battered by shelling and airstrikes,
where a father turned rocket debris
into brightly painted swings.

Where children build their joy
on what aimed for their body's dust.

I heard one girl's laughter swoops
high above the rest, her right
hand missing from a missile
that hit the market.

What do I think we should be doing
about Syria? Imagining until we grieve.
Grieving until we act

like we know what kind of laughter
is the sound of the beginning
of the end of the world.

DAYTIME, SOMEWHERE

I've been thinking about time
and how much you still have to do
and I want you to know no one out here
is any better. We just broke different kinds of rules.

I think the hardest people in the world
to forgive are the people we once were,
the people we are trying desperately to not stir
into the recipe of who we are now.

I've been working to write it all down
in the diary of a good god,
and I'm not sure I'm doing it right,
but I'm doing my best, and I dream

about the day you'll be here
with your suitcase, hanging out
with the sun, learning
how to pack light.

Remember before you went in,
how you couldn't stop
reading the comments
on the news?

Remember the one that said
there wasn't a chance
in hell you could change?
Hell isn't where I place my bets.

There are few weapons more dangerous
than our wounds, and, being wounded,
there are things we all do
that we would often rather die than face.

But no one heals what they refuse to look at.
So when asked if I think you're a good person,
I say, *I don't believe in good people. I believe in people*
who are committed to knowing their own wounds intimately.

And right now I know you're in there
scouring your wound's diary, and I pray
everyone out here is, too, especially whoever might believe
they are telling you the truth

when they tell you what you've done wrong
with your life. Truth doesn't fly that kind of kite.
Truth knows everybody's dark side
is daytime somewhere.

Do you know science just proved an atom
can exist in two places at the same time?
No one is ever only at the scene of their crimes.
Each of us is always also somewhere holy.

You are always with me. I am always with you.

RESENTMENT [VERB]

1.   Loading the past into a cannon
to murder this year.

FIGHT FOR LOVE

Maybe you suggested something unthinkable
like perhaps I should get my dog groomed

after she rolled in the poo of a sick horse
and I naturally concluded you were the absolute worst

for thinking I would subject an angel to the horror
of being bathed by a blade-toting stranger.

Maybe it was when you were editing my book,
and you said something elitist like,

You can't end every poem by repeating the last line,
or, *You can't have the word 'moon' or 'firefly'*

in every piece you write, and I screamed something like,
I'D RATHER HAVE A SKY WITHOUT A MOON IN IT

THAN A POEM WITHOUT A MOON IN IT, YOU UPPITY
THESAURUS-ADDICTED SNOW GLOBE FULL OF DANDRUFF.

Maybe it was the poly argument, your face going fire-engine red
the second I mentioned an old flame.

Maybe I decided you didn't want history to exist,
which meant you wanted me to be magic,

a virgin rabbit pulled out of your pretty hat—
or a lady cut in half.

Maybe it was when you said *like* six times
in a single sentence and I freaked out about our age difference

and you said I couldn't argue for my own time-earned wisdom
while throwing a 3-year-old's tantrum. Good point.

Maybe it was one of the times I got so mad
I defriended you on Facebook, and you got so mad

about that I decided you were the shallow end
of the baby pool. Maybe you peed in the water

to prove me right. Maybe it was the night
at the straight bar when the table of men

invited you to sit with them.
Maybe it was when you didn't notice their eyes

drooling down your breasts, thought Celine Dion
on the karaoke machine was just bringing them to tears.

Maybe it was when you suggested the bar was queer-friendly
because someone asked if I was Tegan and Sara.

Maybe it was one of those nights
when I was two people, neither of them the real me,

just caricatures of my worst possible qualities.
Maybe it was when we decided to start a podcast

discussing all of our arguments,
then got into an argument during the first five minutes

of recording and cancelled the show,
but at some point it hit me:

You and I are always going to fight
for love. I am always going to drag my heart

into the ring to call you the knockout
I've been waiting for my whole life.

You are always going to trigger me
into rifling through my history

until every ghost is hunted out.
Every fight we have ever had has been an opportunity

to unbruise the past. What hurt would we still be
hoarding in our garage had we never fought

about your inability to park a car because the GPS
stops telling you what to do when you pull into a driveway?

Please run over the mailbox if that keeps me
looking for new ways to send my best self to you.

I am so in love with who we are,
who we have been fighting to become together.

I can't believe I finally adore a human
as much as I adore my dog.

Even when I'm in the doghouse
I like know you like love me like so much.

Thank you for saying there's no need
to open our relationship because being with me

is already like being with fifty
impossible people. Thank you for accepting

my friend request for the fifth time this year.
Thank you for screaming

all the way home from that straight bar
to the bed where our bodies made up

while the moon flew through the window,
and a firefly poured into the room

and landed in your hand, which you opened
like a ring box and asked me to marry you,

and we were so new, I blushed
instead of answered.

But a firefly is forever and you know what my answer is.
A firefly is forever and you know what my answer is.

LETTER TO THE EDITOR

I.
There was a typo in the book.
The line read, *I want to merry you.*
But *merry* was spelled M-E-R-R-Y.
I thought, That's what I want to do—
merry somebody until their blush
paints the town red.

II.

Years ago I went home with a woman
and right before our lips met for the first time,
she jumped up out of the bed, ran to her closet,
and grabbed a stethoscope. She put the earpieces in my ears,
slipped the knob down her shirt onto her heart and whispered,
I want you to listen to my heart speed up when you kiss me.
I kissed her and I listened as it beat faster and faster.
I gave her an apple when I left.
She kept the seeds and has called me
Johnny ever since.
But we didn't live happily ever after.

III.
When I was a kid I had an imaginary friend named Johnny.
He did all the bad stuff. He spilled my father's ashtray
on the white living room rug. He paid Tim Willindanger 25 cents
to pee in his own hands. He snuck into Julie Hill's toy room
and ripped the eyeballs off of all of her favorite teddy bears.
He called Beth Hayword a stupid poop. (She was a stupid poop).

IV.
If you have an imaginary friend as an adult,
there's a good chance you need a whole lot of therapy.
I had been paying my therapist's mortgage since 2004.
Johnny had dated everyone I have ever loved.

V.

You were behind me in line at the coffee shop,
and you heard me place my order, and you said,
I don't think that's your drink. I think
you've been a long time ordering the wrong kind.

VI.

The first night I touched you
I swore to never touch you again
until I'd had spent an entire year
pulling every button from the shirts on my back
and sewing new eyes for the teddy bears.

VII.

You're my favorite editor.
You're the only person in my whole life
who has ever convinced me I could spell *marry* with an *E*
and it could still also mean forever.

VIII.

These are my vows:

—Johnny Appleseed, whose real name was Johnny Chapman,
 was someone who would never hurt a fly.
 So much so that if he spotted even one mosquito
 flying too close to a flame, he would jump up
 and put out his own campfire on even the coldest darkest nights.
 (That's the type of Johnny I intend to be.)

—The heartbeat is actually the sound made
 by the heart valves closing.
 If you, my love, ever hold a stethoscope to my chest,
 I will tell you to listen for the silence in between.
 What is and what will always be yours
 is the sound of my heart
 finally opening.

LIVING PROOF

I have a few happy friends.
I ask them about being happy
the same way my high school friends
ask me about being gay, *So, what
do you people do exactly? How do you do IT?*

Their answers are never as freaky
as I would hope. Almost always they answer god
or booze. One I don't tolerate.
The other, I'm told,
doesn't tolerate me.

I'm fascinated with this idea
of getting high on life. I imagine people
on their backs in lilac fields snorting the lines
the planes leave in the sky, waking
with honeymoons in their bloodstreams.

Me, I often feel like I'm the vaccine
for goosebumps. I can't remember the last time
someone commented on my sunny disposition.
That doesn't mean I haven't tried to juice
the sun for every holy drop.

No one stands by passively
while their joy gets lost in the dark.
I know it is its own injury,
spending too much of your life
just holding yourself together—

I've known that since the first time
I tried to die: I was too ashamed to go back
and get the stitches out on time so they scarred

as badly as the wound. It's the one part of me
I never stop thinking ugly—twenty tiny holes

framing a would-be flatline I still can't look at
without seeing the light going out
in my best friend's eyes while she watched
the doctor's needle close the letter
I swore to never send.

The last, and I mean the last time,
I tried to return myself to sender
was a year ago this June.
After five months so sick I was certain
my stomach would never know a butterfly again,

I got so low I had to look up
to see rock bottom, and, ghosted by hope,
I got in my car and started driving toward
a dead end, a cliff that had been my back-up plan
if ever the pain got stronger than I am.

Now I gotta let you know—this is a true story.
On my way to the end that day, I was already mostly gone,
clumps of my own hair covering the dashboard
from me failing to weed the hell from my mind.
I was sobbing and snaking around my own neck,

when I looked up from the steering wheel
and saw a stranger above me on the overpass—
holding on to the wrong side of the rail with one hand,
his arm was taut as a kite string about to lift his body
into the air and fly

into four rows of traffic.
This stranger and I had the same idea,
but as soon as I saw him, my eyes locked on him

like two screeching red lights that couldn't stop begging,
STOP STOP STOP STOP.

I was the last car to pass before the fire trucks
and ambulances raced to clot the vein of traffic,
to tourniquet the road, so when the man jumped
his death, his body wouldn't graveyard
the windshield of someone driving home

with their baby in the backseat. I watched
rescue workers run to try to talk him off the ledge
while I shot out of my car behind the overpass
and started circling in the madness of being a twister
praying for someone else's sun to not go down,

pacing in the mind mangle of being someone
on my way to die stopping to tell somebody else not to.
I might never know if he saw me, but I was haunting
the ground, punching my hands into the tornado
of my grief to grab each piece of my own lost mind

so I could get my footing long enough
to clearly ask the air beneath this man
to catch him like a snowflake on the tongue.
A tongue that might also whisper, *Sweet sweet soul,*
heaven is in the other direction.

Please don't make gravity play god.
I've heard there are fields—acres of lilacs like petalled purple hearts
blooming only to pull us through and all you have to do is holler
your name into a canyon and hear
someone else's name echo back.

Never in my life did I want more
to keep my blood blue, did I want more to live

than when I looked up and saw myself in someone else
trying to become the sky. I didn't even know him,
but I know it would have killed me to watch him die.

So at 12:31 PM, when he decided not to—
when he came down, when the road opened—
I did, too, my whole world, my whole mind
went home with living proof
of what I'd only before known in theory:

that we are truly not alone in this,
that our veins are absolutely strings
tied to other people's kites,
that our lives are that connected.
That my butterflies are never gone,

they're just flying around
in someone else's belly sometimes.
I pray right now they're with that stranger,
I pray he's goosebumped
with a mountain range of joy.

I pray he's high on the long line rivered across the country
of his open palm held out the window
while driving and singing along
to a stranger's favorite song he suddenly knows
all the words to but doesn't know why.

FIRST LOVE

I don't think I ever really kissed
any boys. I think my tongue had
just been punching their tongues.

But as soon as you loved me
all my callous went away.
My hands so soft it hurt to pray.

You'd pick me up at my Catholic college
and I'd sleep for hours until we reached your house.
The first time in my life I'd ever rested,

the first time I didn't have to play a role
I'd never really wanted to get.
That's the medicine it is

to be finally seen by someone.
I'd crack a smile and you'd point to my chest
and say, *What just broke?*

I'd throw my body in the river
but you'd say my name right
and I'd become a stone that skipped.

Do you remember the first record
where we didn't have to change
the pronouns to sing along? We'd gone

so many years without music
that knew us. Music that knew you
could arch your back and I'd have proof

that the earth was round.
Bless who we were then.
Bless who we still are.

My straight friends tease me
because all my best friends
are my ex loves,

but a wise heart told me
it's the most tender part
of queerness—how we've all lost

so much family when we find people
we call family, we'll do almost anything
to not let go. Thank goodness

for the ice storm that trapped us
in that cheap hotel where I drank an entire bottle
of something awful,

and with my fisherman's accent
that I hadn't yet chased away, I finally told you
I'd loved you since we were 15

playing basketball under the street lights
beside the poorest part of the sea.
The ice storm froze the world outside

into a photograph of the past
while I kneeled down and kissed
my future onto your kneecaps.

Two decades talking to Jesus.
That was the first time
I heard him talk back.

Months later, church bells ringing
through my dorm room, I wrote my senior thesis
about you and no one knew

how hard I was praying
to stop hiding myself in metaphor,
to be brave enough to carve the truth

into the chapel door.
Only you can imagine
how much time I spent

picking out my outfit the night
you took me to my first queer bar
in Portland, Maine--the biggest city

I'd ever walked through. I was so excited
and so scared that we'd be spotted,
or killed, on our way inside,

we sat in the parking lot
for over an hour till I changed my mind
and you drove me home,

mascara pouring down
my brand new boy shirt.
I couldn't

have guessed there'd ever come a time
like the winter we traveled to Blue Hill
to visit your mother.

Asleep when we arrived after midnight,
she'd lit our room with candles and rested
a joint in the center of the bed.

Neither of us were any good at smoking
but we pulled her welcome into our lungs
like it was one hundred years of oxygen.

Up until then we didn't know
anyone in the world
would celebrate us

wiping the steam from the glass
to see each other blushing
in the same bathroom mirror in the morning.

I was thinking about that a few months ago
when I was invited back to my catholic college
to read my poems for the first time.

You, in the front row,
near the nuns and the school president
and the teacher who had given me an A

on the manuscript
I had been too terrified
to write your name in.

Mandy, I know so much has not gotten easier.
I know so much has not gotten better, but
that moment knocked the wind out of me--Time

finally being the kind of father we all deserve.
The world turning its porch light on for us.
It was so bright

I could feel the freckles
on my 15-year-old face
warming in its glow.

I could feel hope
traveling backward
to find us,

to whisper into our chests,
There will be music for you
one day.

ACKNOWLEDGEMENTS

Thank you to Megan Falley for trying, without success, to keep me writing "in the world of the poem." Thank you to Sonya Renee and The Body Is Not An Apology for inspiring Boomerang Valentine. Thank you to Like Taylor Like Mali for somehow making his way into my queer love poem. Thank you to Dr. Julie Colwell. Thank you to Dr. Daniel Kinderlehrer. Thank you to Squash, My Beating Heart With Fur and Legs. Thank you to my sister—I love you as big as the Atlantic.

ABOUT THE AUTHOR

Winner of the first ever Women of the World Poetry Slam in 2008, Andrea Gibson remains one of the most captivating performers in the spoken word poetry scene today. Known for pulling hearts out of chests to either wrench or kiss, Gibson has authored four full-length collections of poems, an illustrated book of their most memorable quotes (Take Me With You, Penguin 2018), and has released seven beloved albums. Gibson regularly sells out 500+ capacity standing room only venues to eager audiences, mouthing along every word, further popularizing the art form and creating a space for each person in the room to feel, and to heal. In a fierce oscillation between activism and love, Andrea's most recent literary triumph, Lord of the Butterflies (Button Poetry, 2018), is a book of protests, panic attacks, and pride parades. These poems riot against gun violence, homophobia, and white supremacy, while jubilating gender expansion, queer love, and the will to stay alive.

OTHER BOOKS BY THE AUTHOR

You Better Be Lightning
Take Me With You
How Poetry Can Change Your Heart
Lord of the Butterflies: Writing Prompts & Stories
the madness vase
PANSY
Pole Dancing To Gospel Hymns

BUTTON POETRY BEST SELLERS

Neil Hilborn, *Our Numbered Days*
Hanif Abdurraqib, *The Crown Ain't Worth Much*
Sabrina Benaim, *Depression & Other Magic Tricks*
Rudy Francisco, *Helium*
Rachel Wiley, *Nothing Is Okay*
Neil Hilborn, *The Future*
Phil Kaye, *Date & Time*
Andrea Gibson, *Lord of the Butterflies*
Blythe Baird, *If My Body Could Speak*
Andrea Gibson, *You Better Be Lightning*

Available at buttonpoetry.com/shop and more!

OTHER BOOKS BY BUTTON POETRY

If you enjoyed this book, please consider checking out some of our others, below. Readers like you allow us to keep broadcasting and publishing. Thank you!

Available at buttonpoetry.com/shop and more!